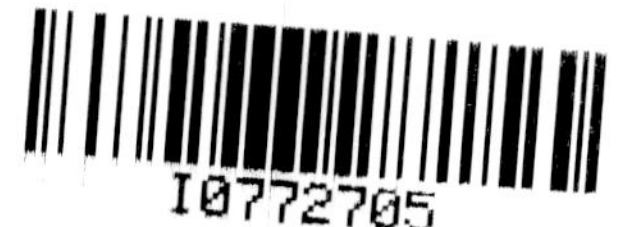

Coloring book for adults and kids 35 dog image for design

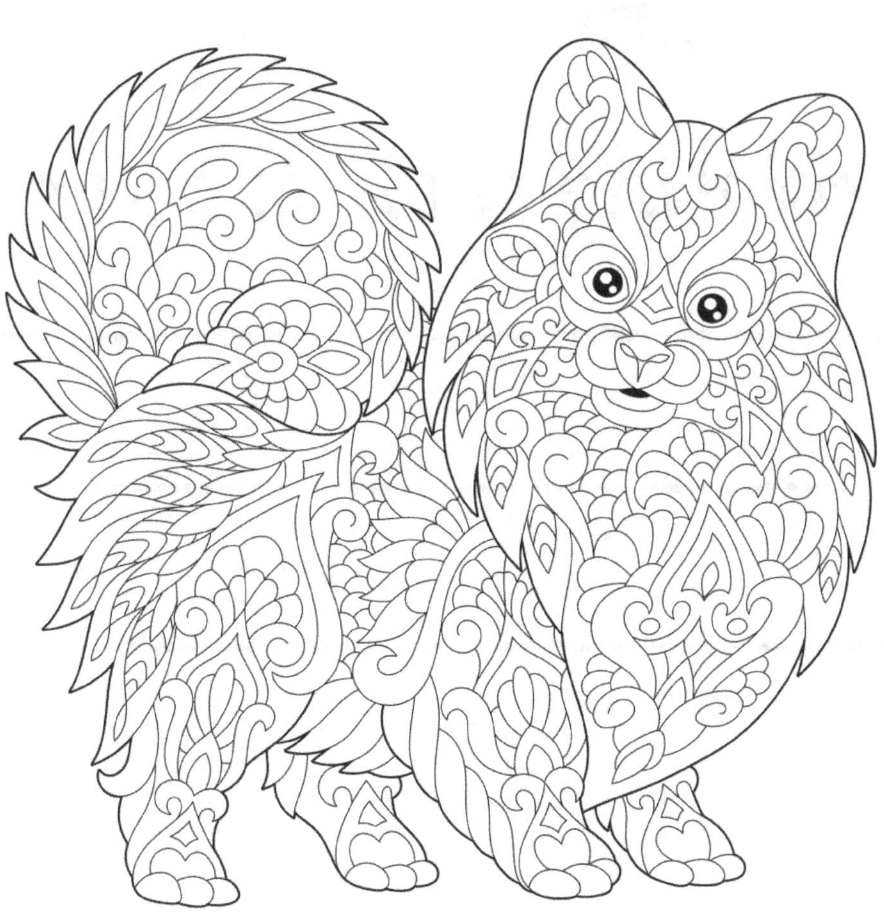

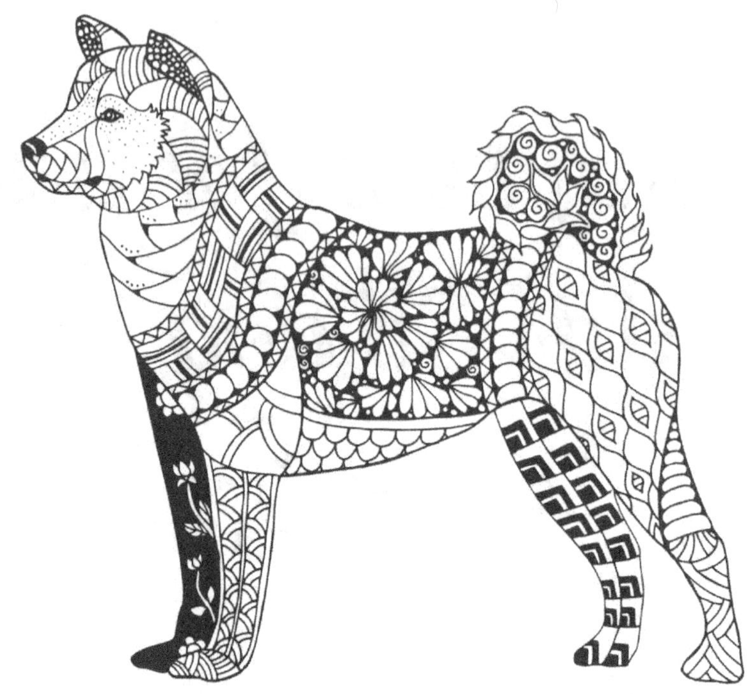

This coloring book is belongs to

____

____

____

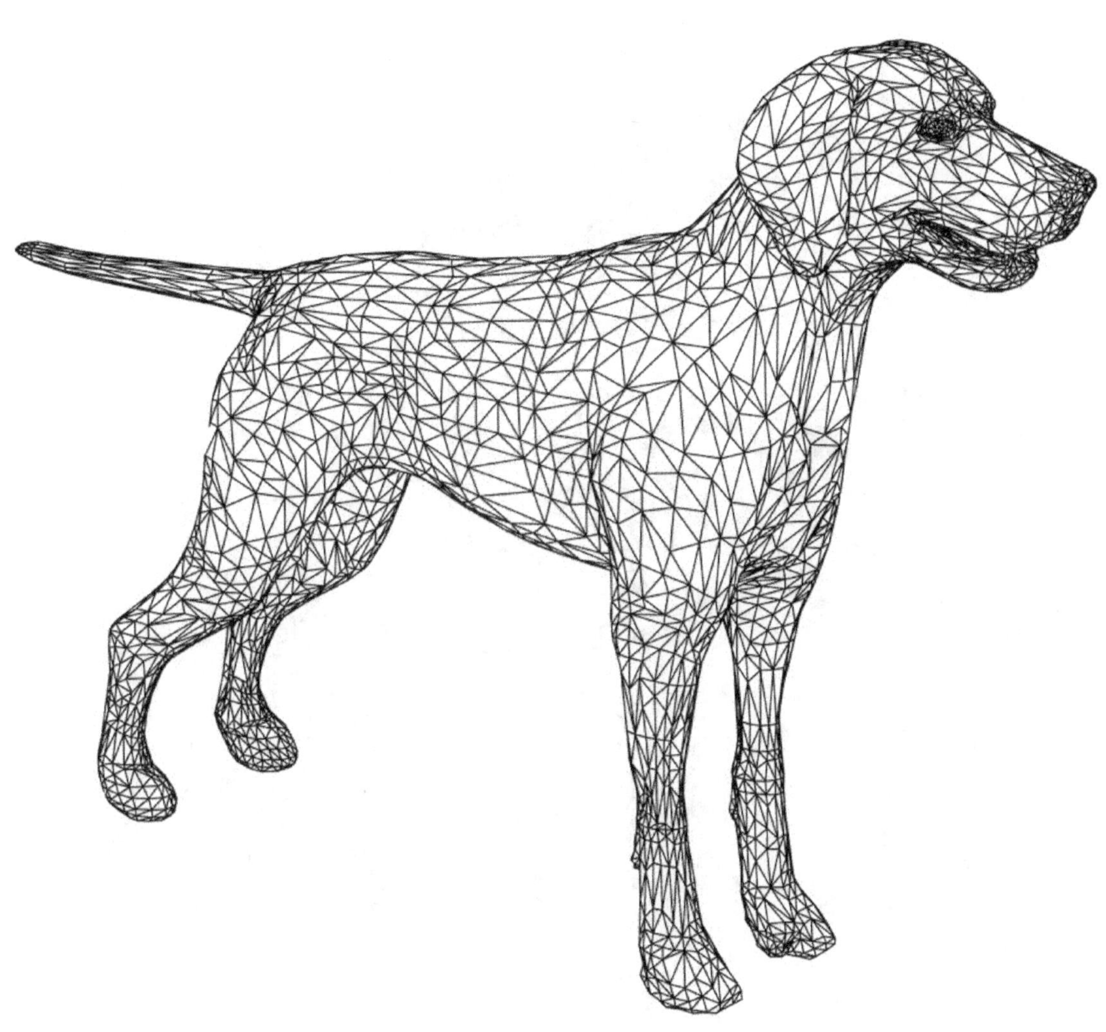

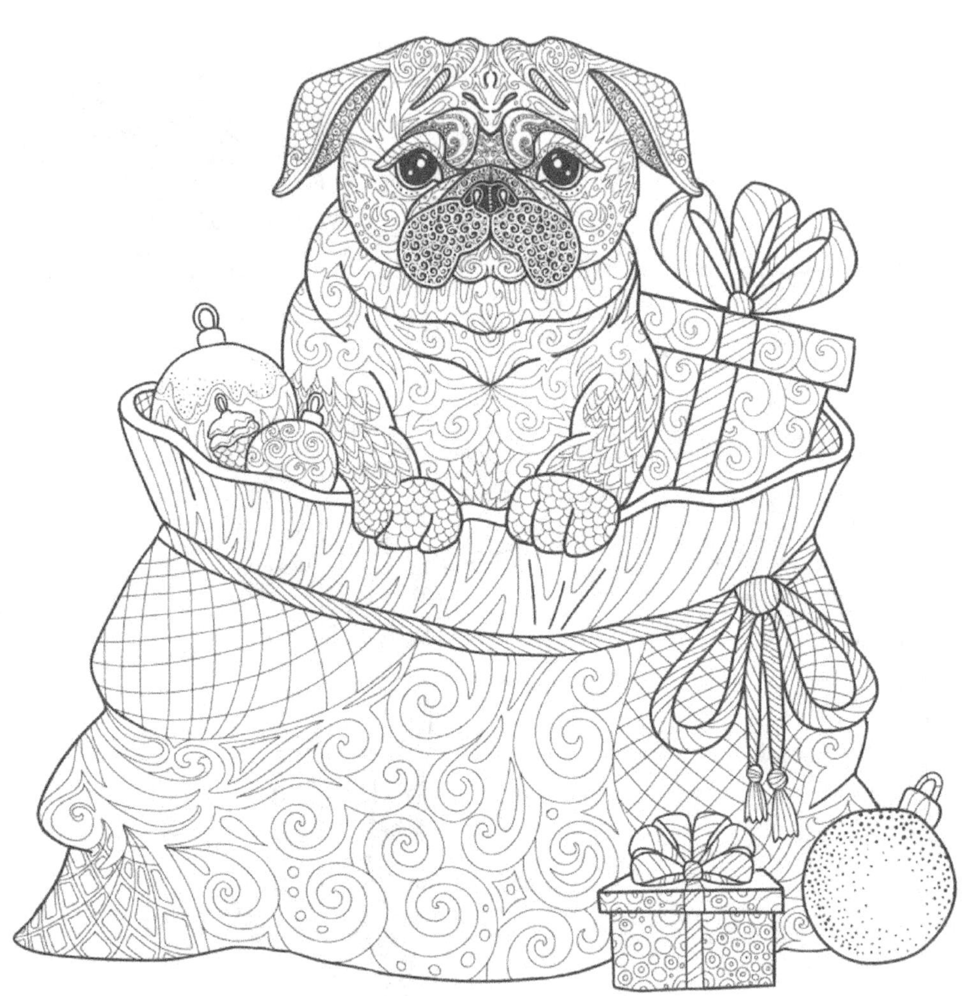

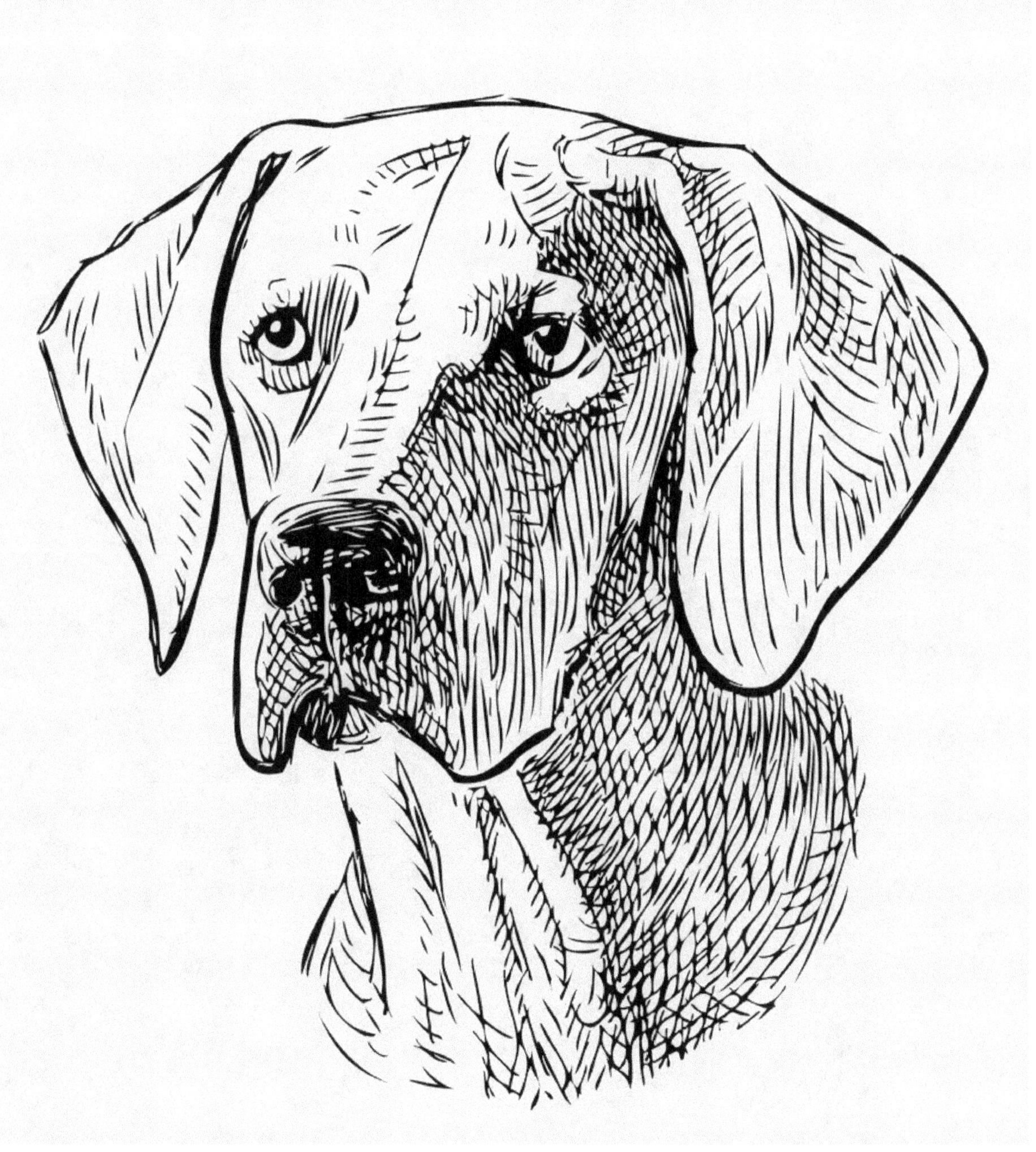

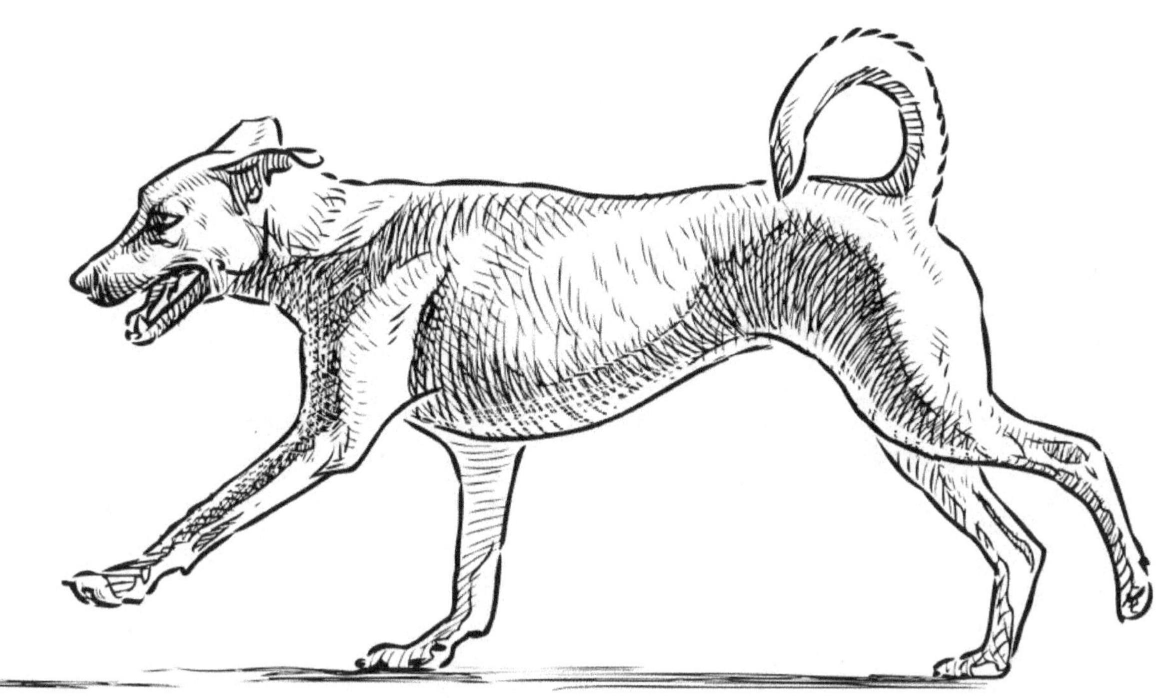

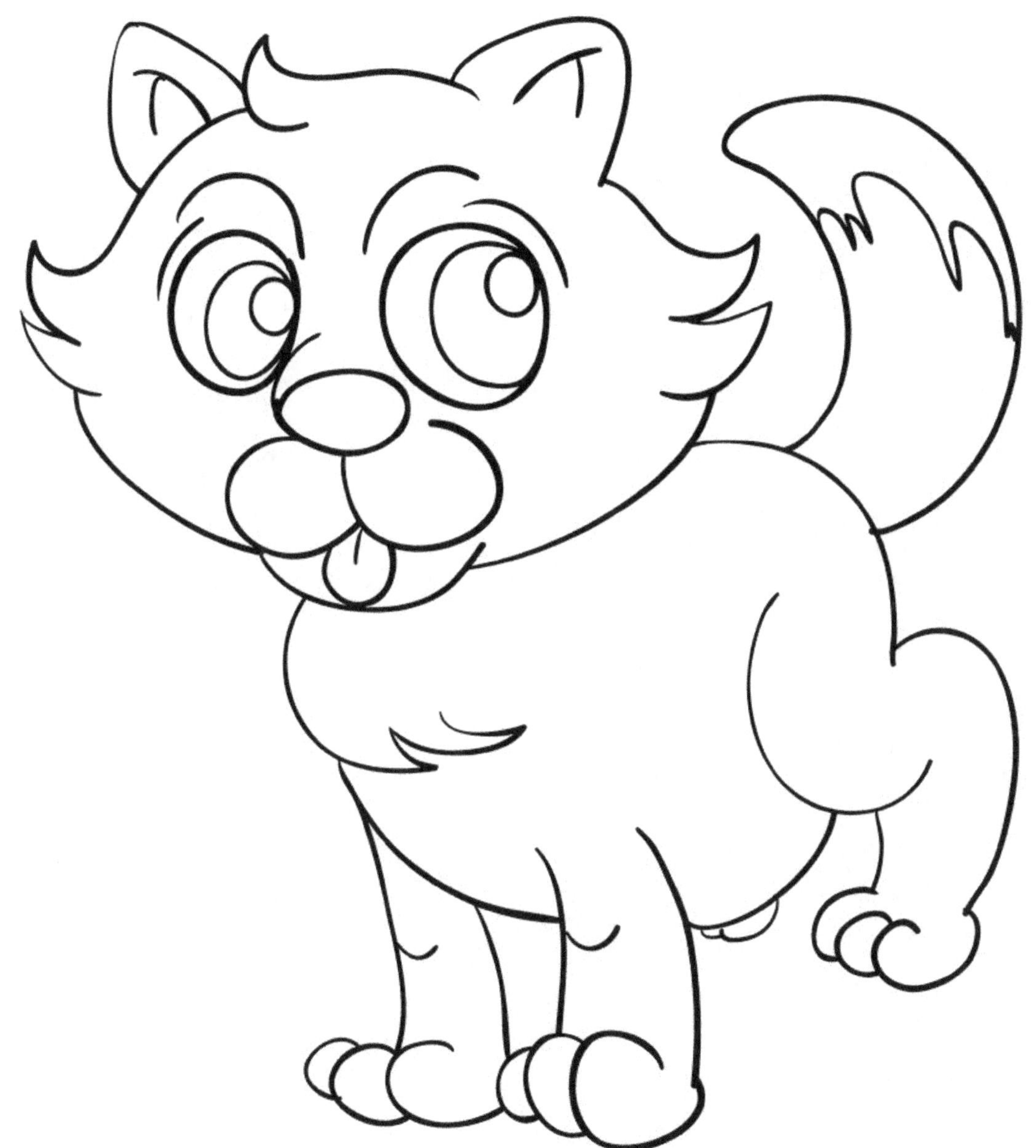

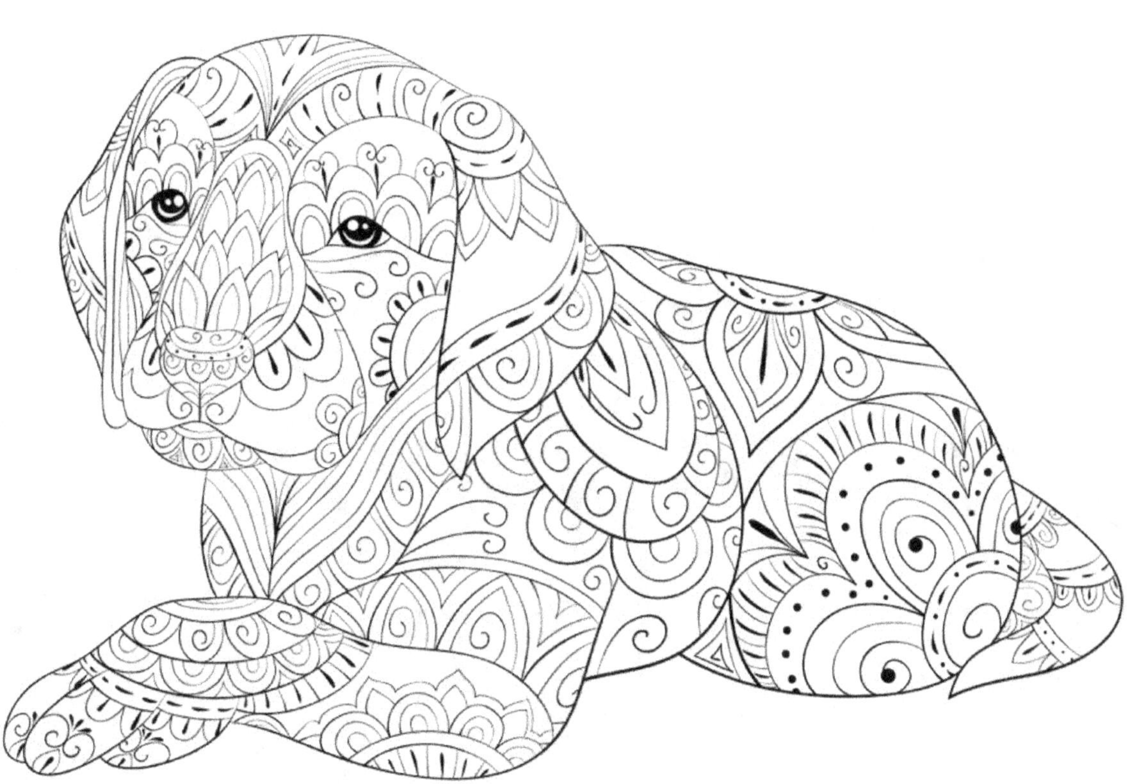

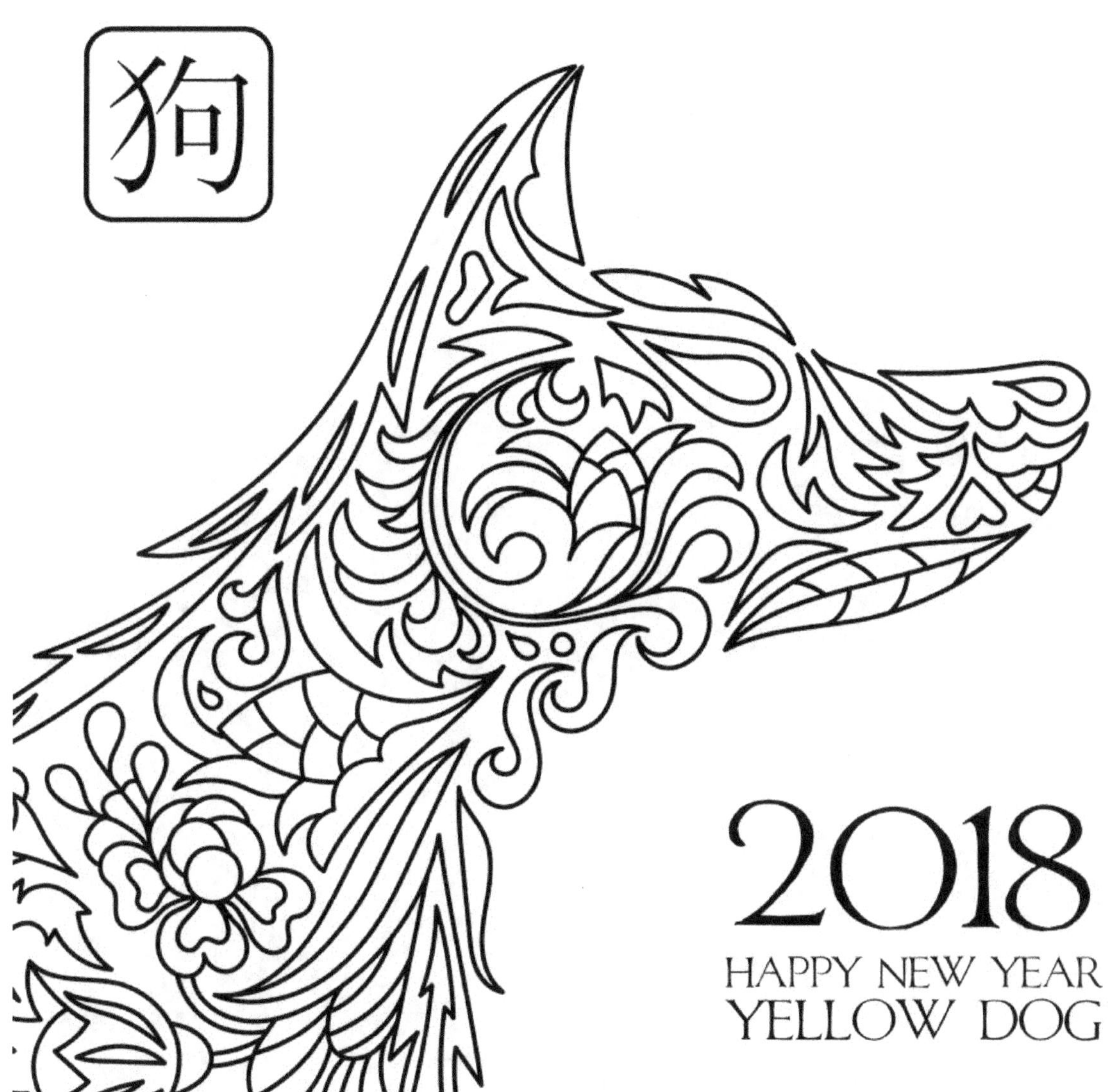
狗
2018
HAPPY NEW YEAR
YELLOW DOG

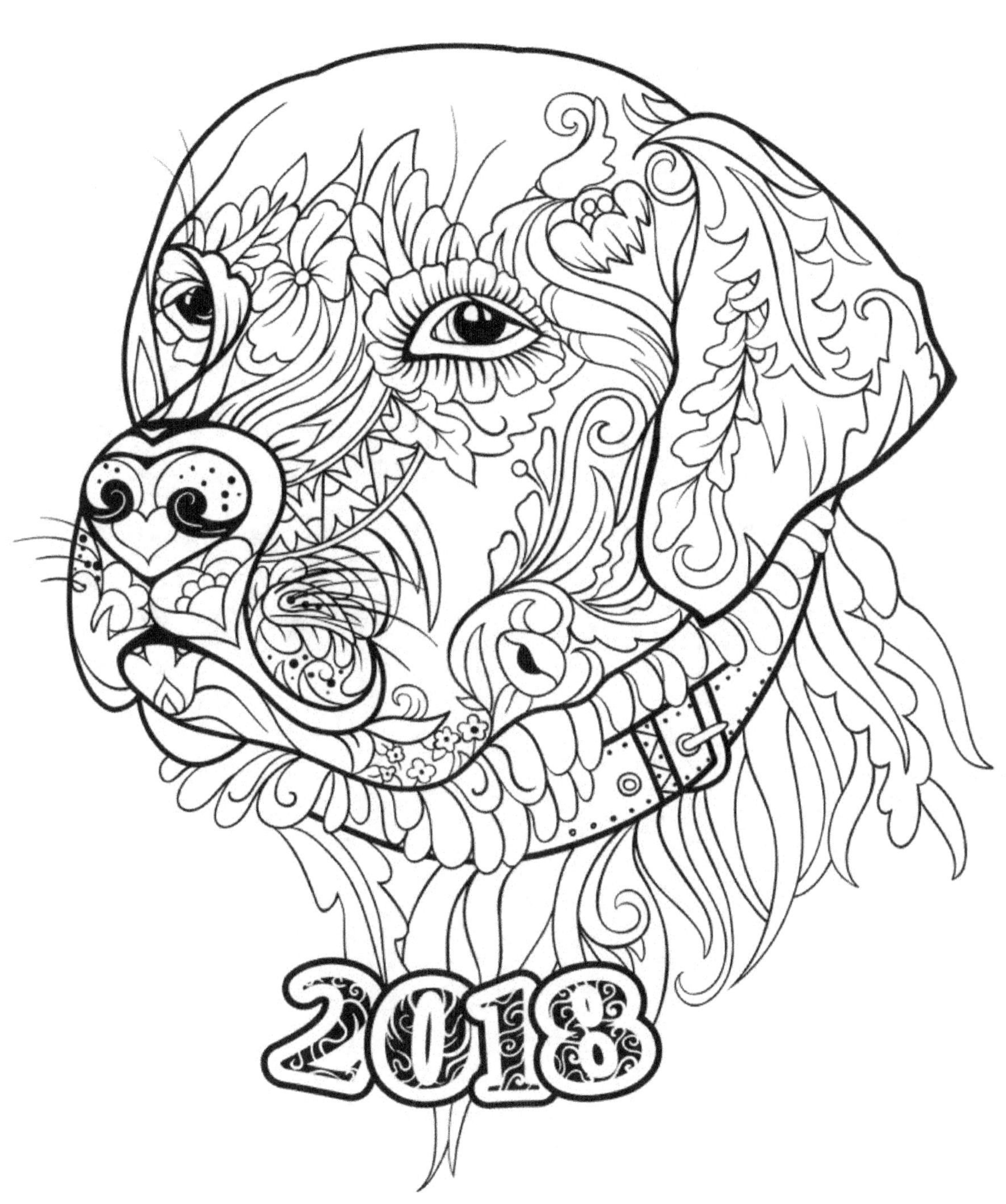

2018

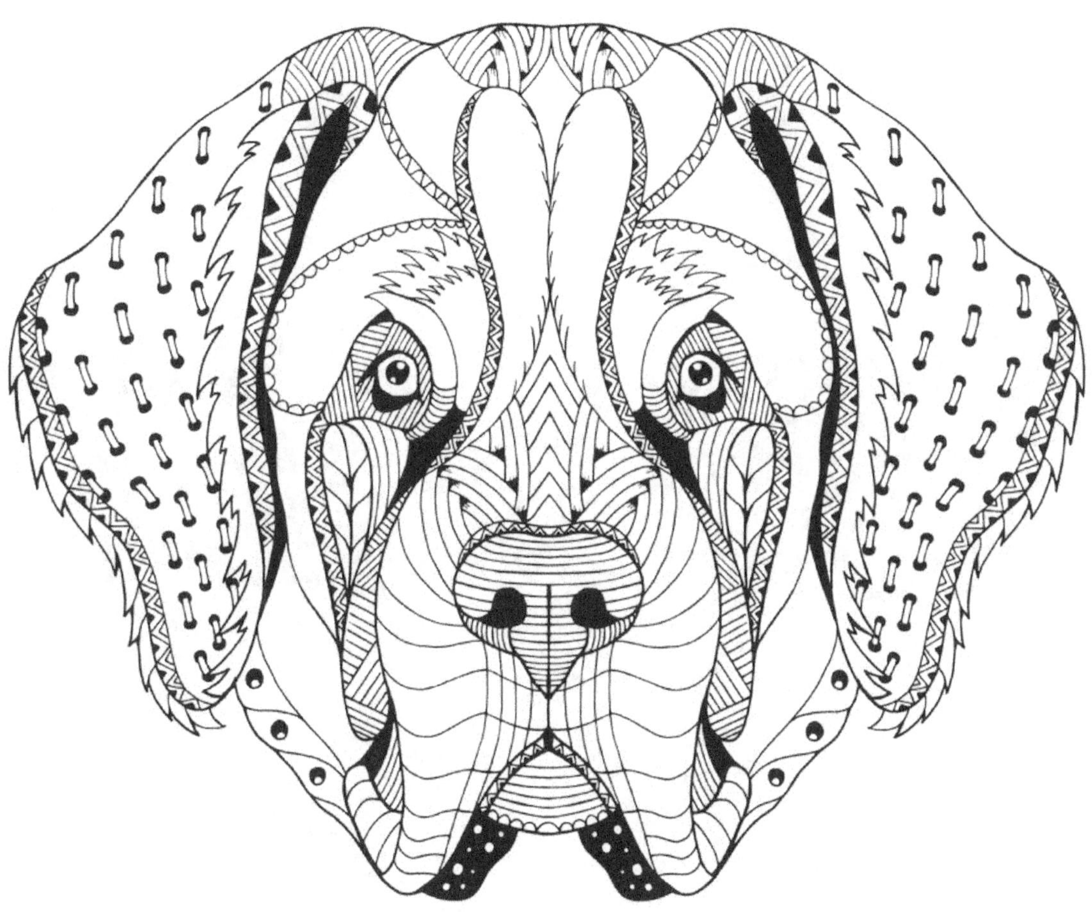

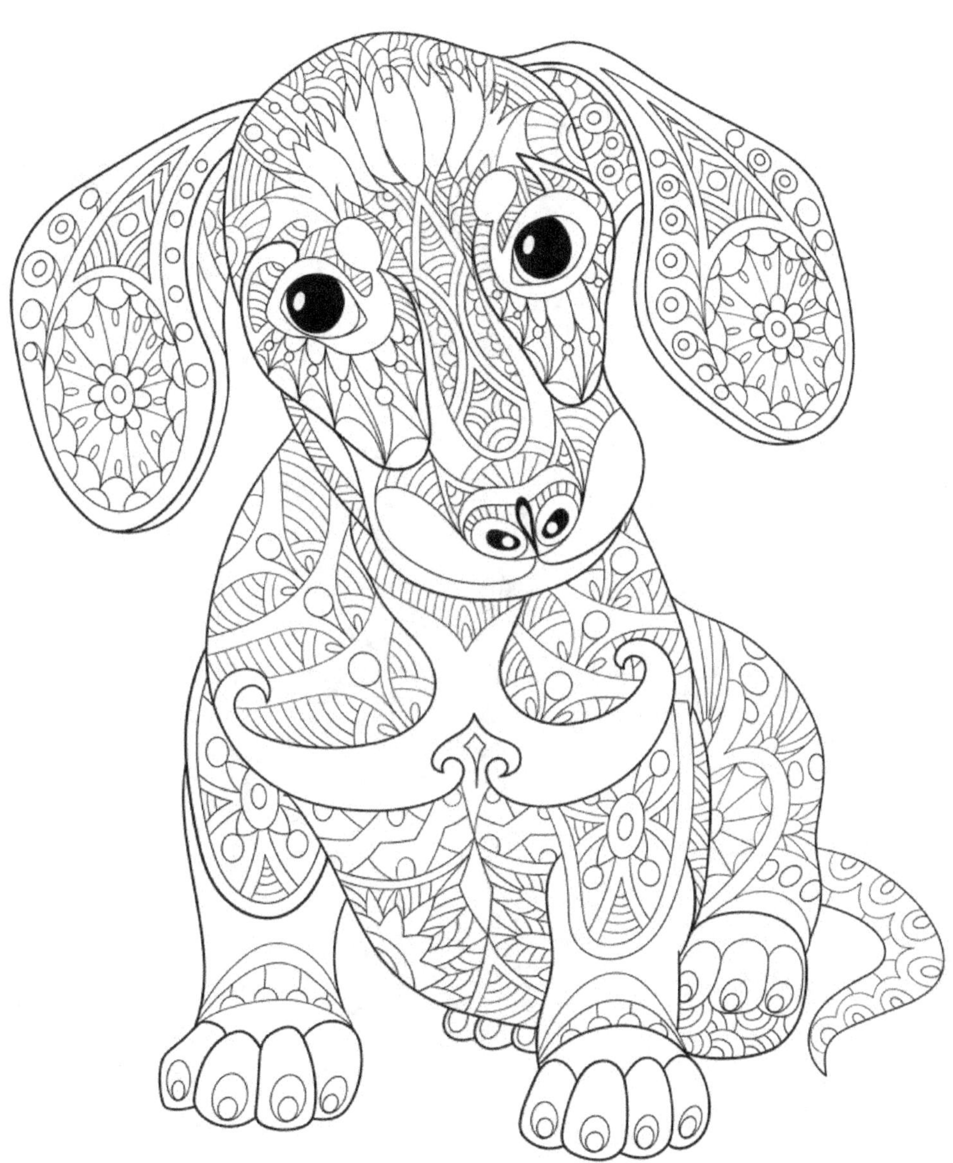

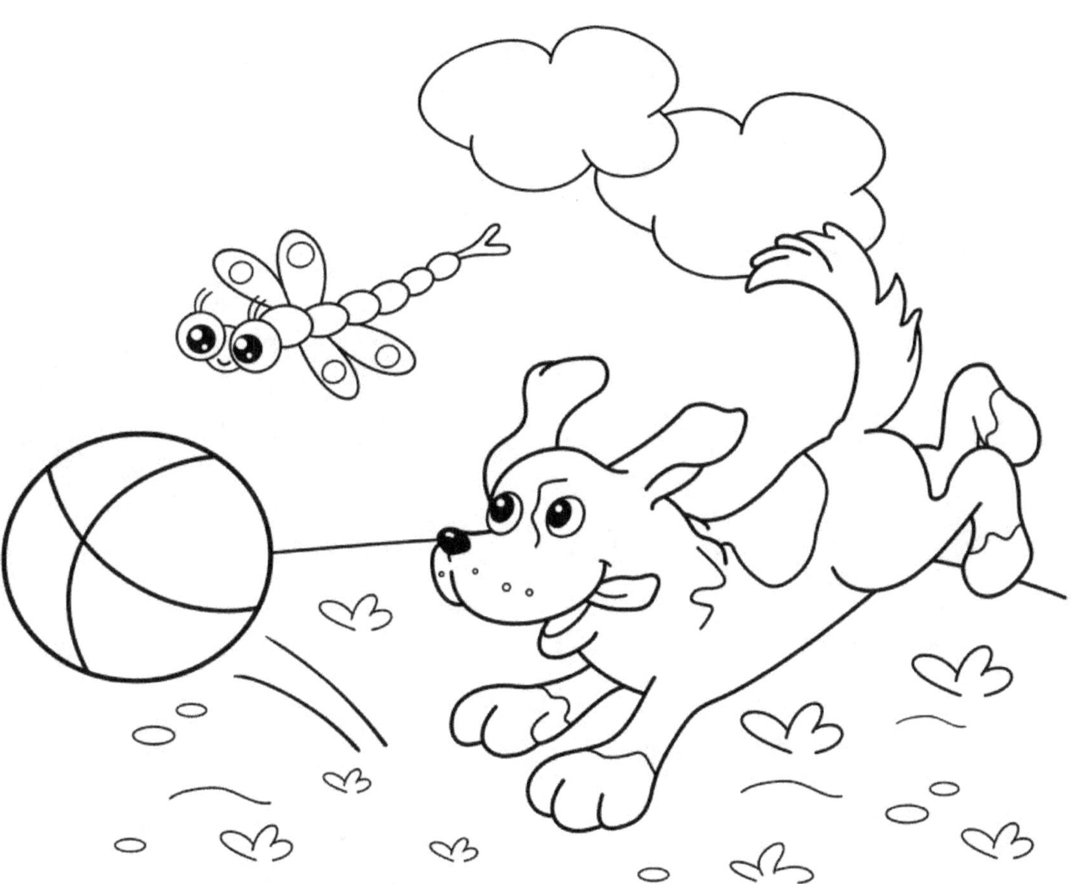

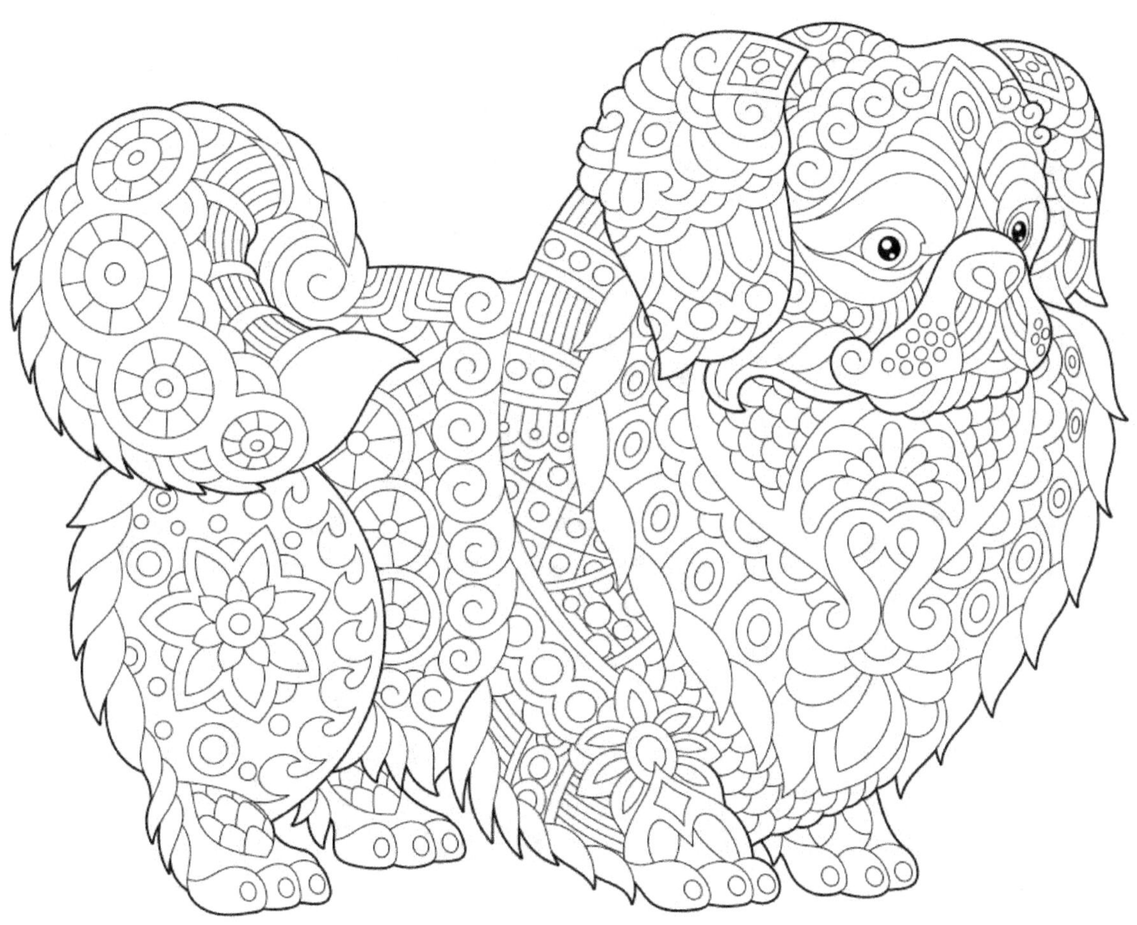

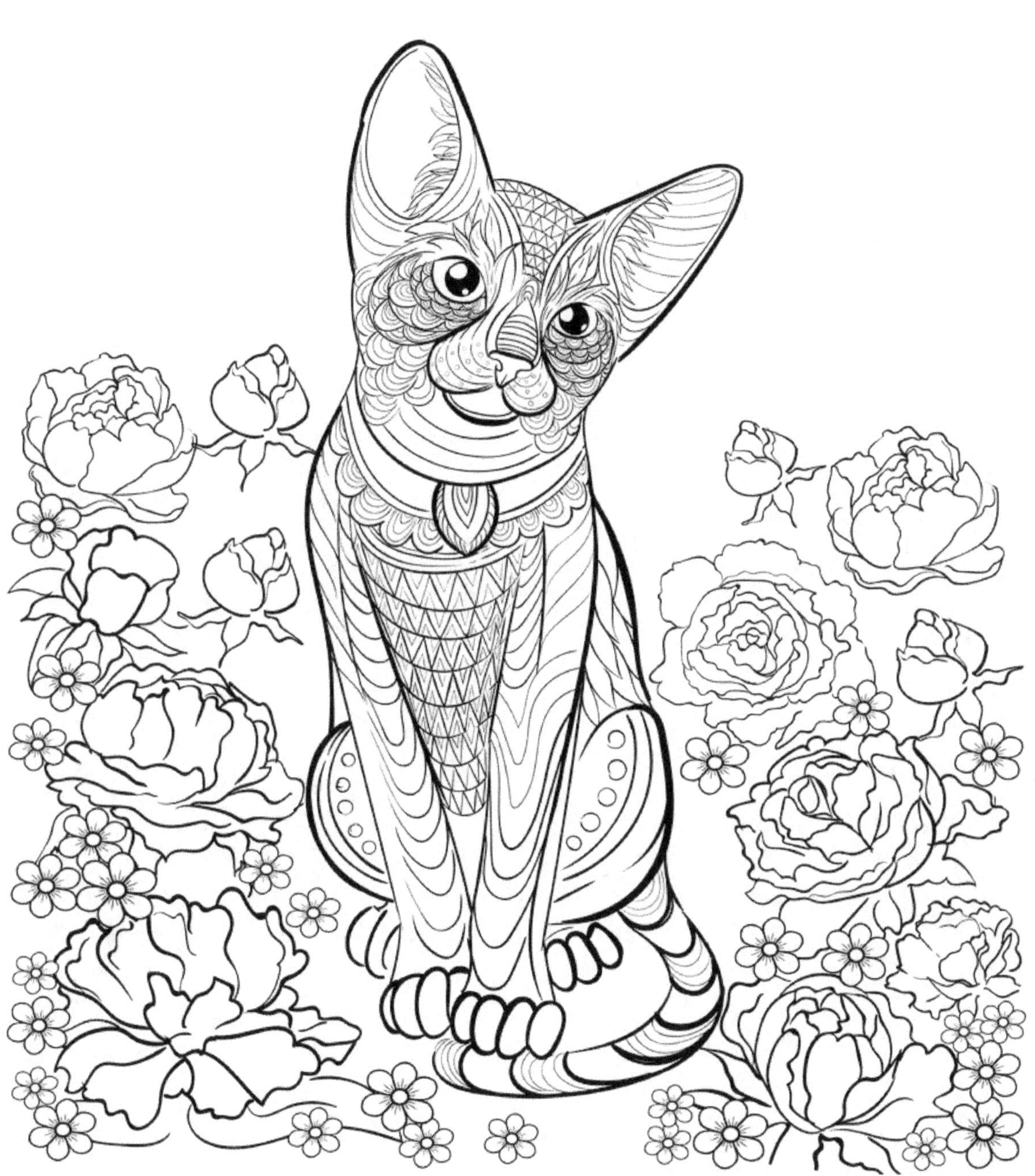

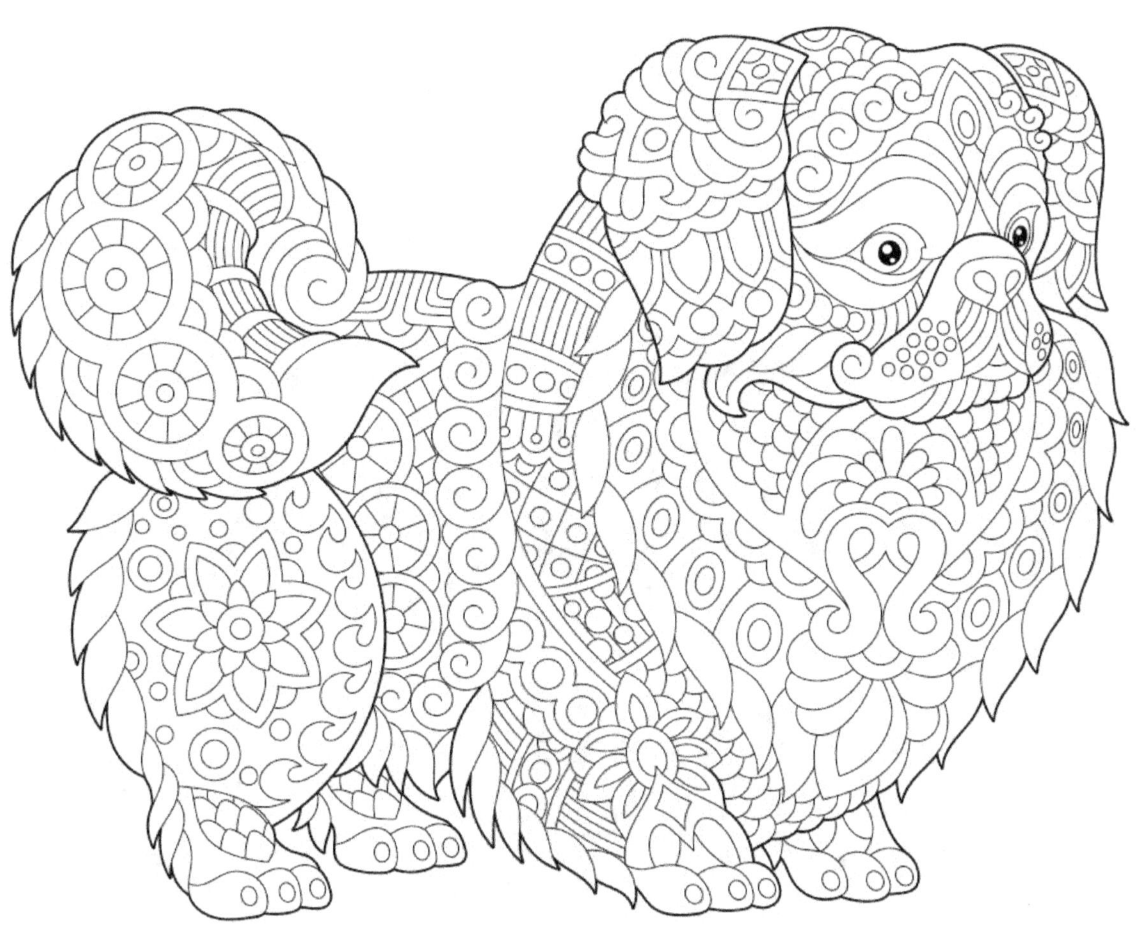

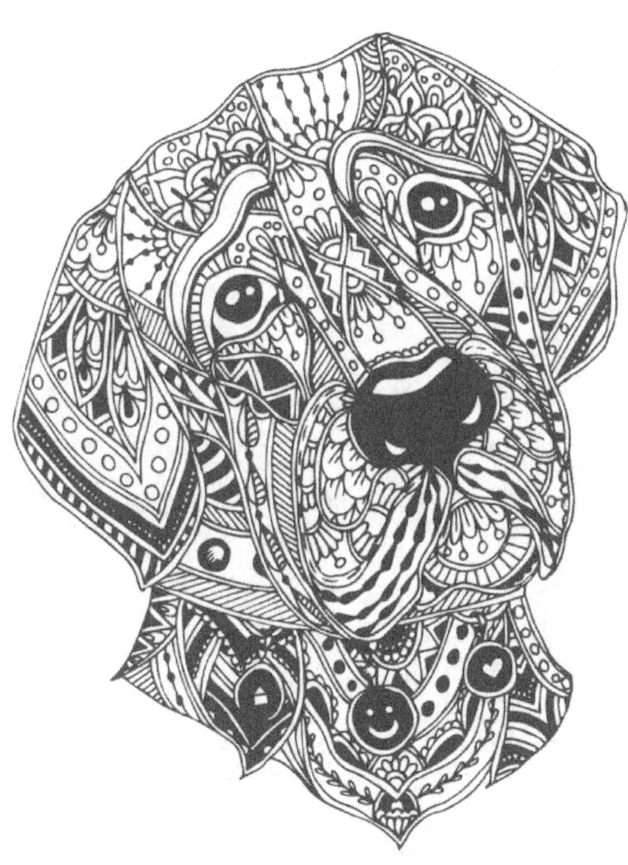

Dog

friend of human

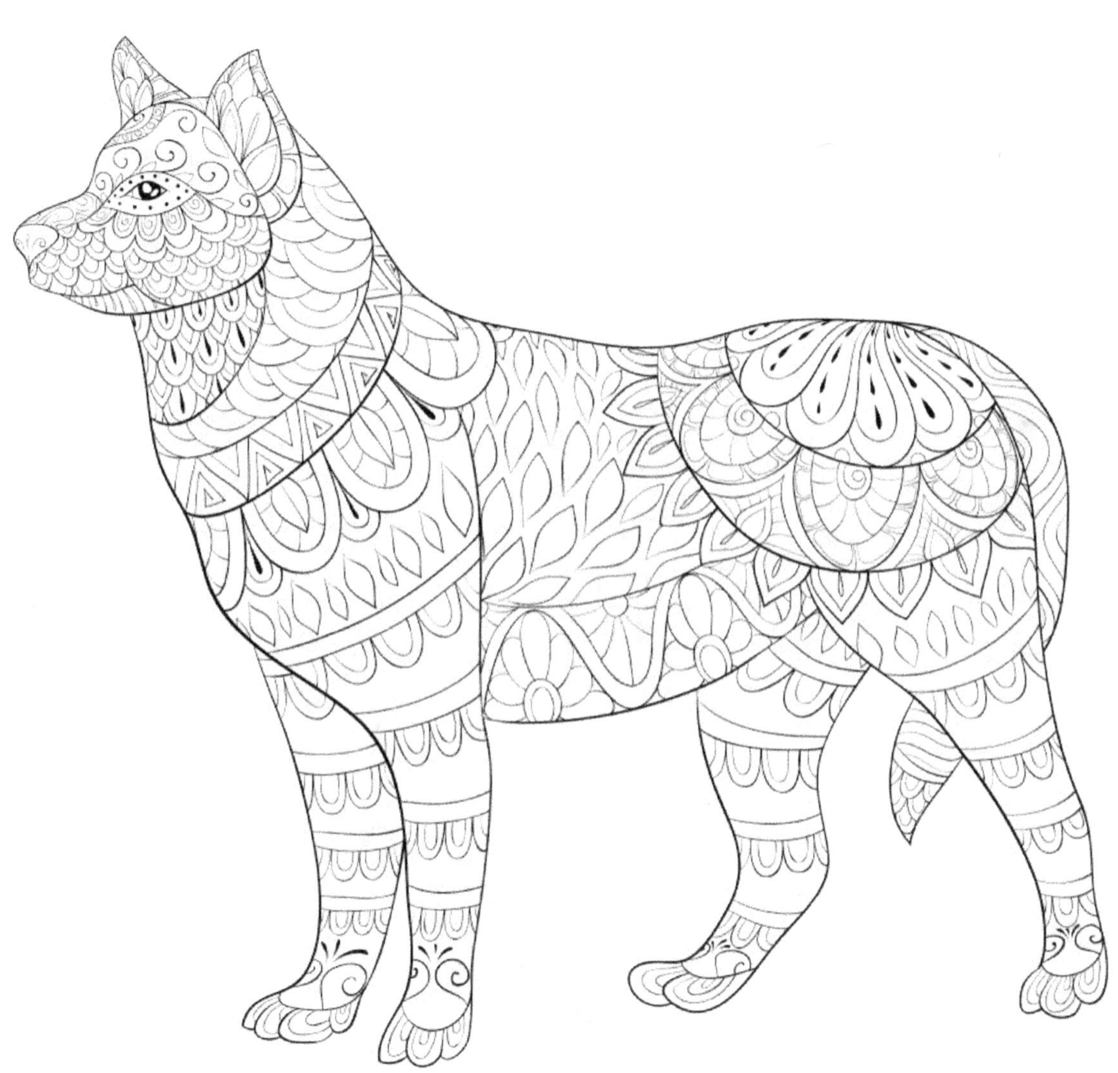

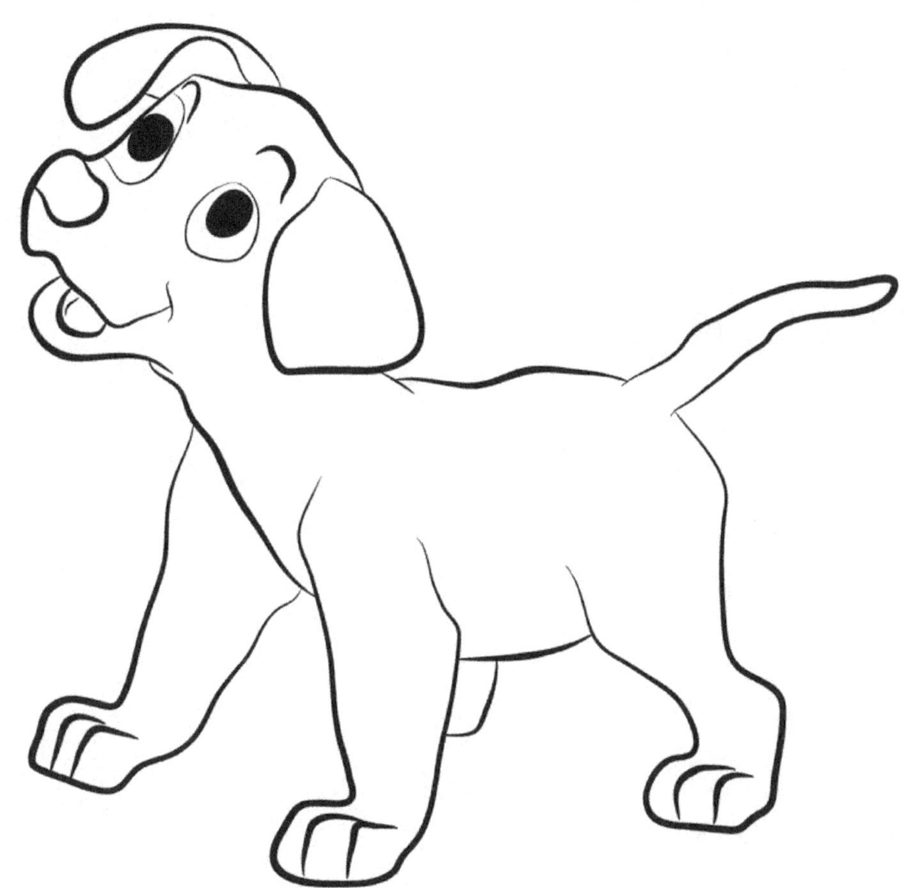

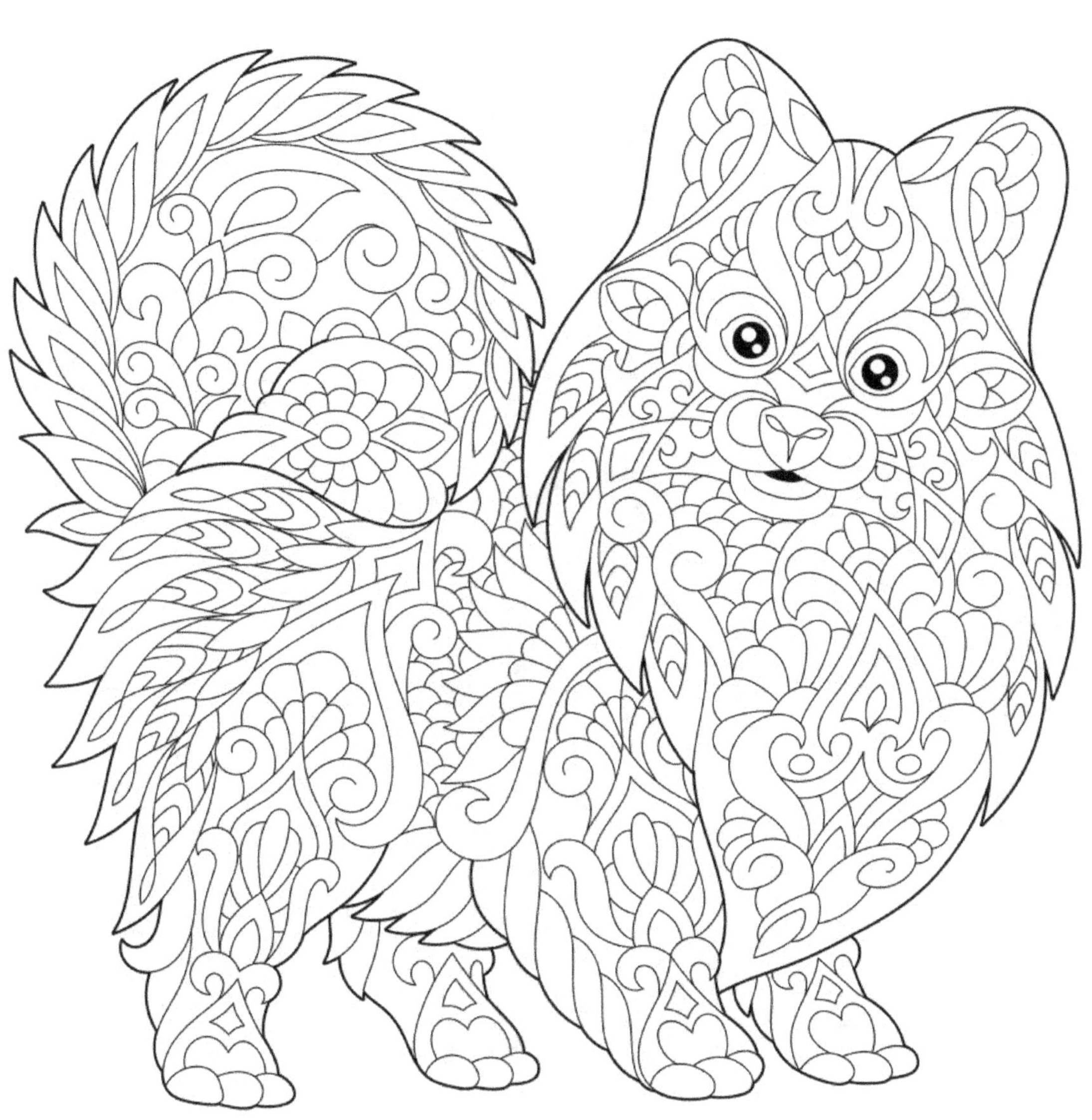

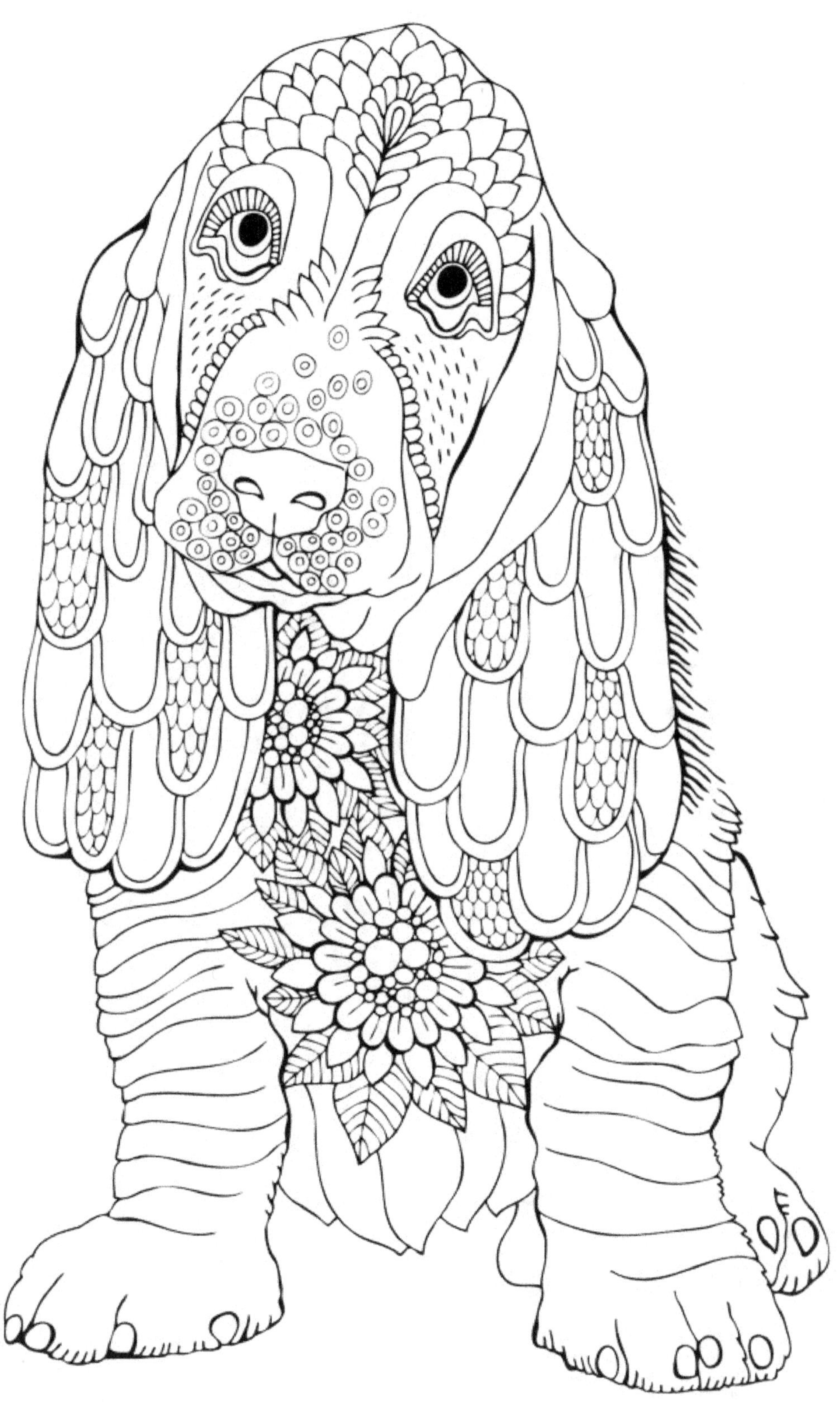

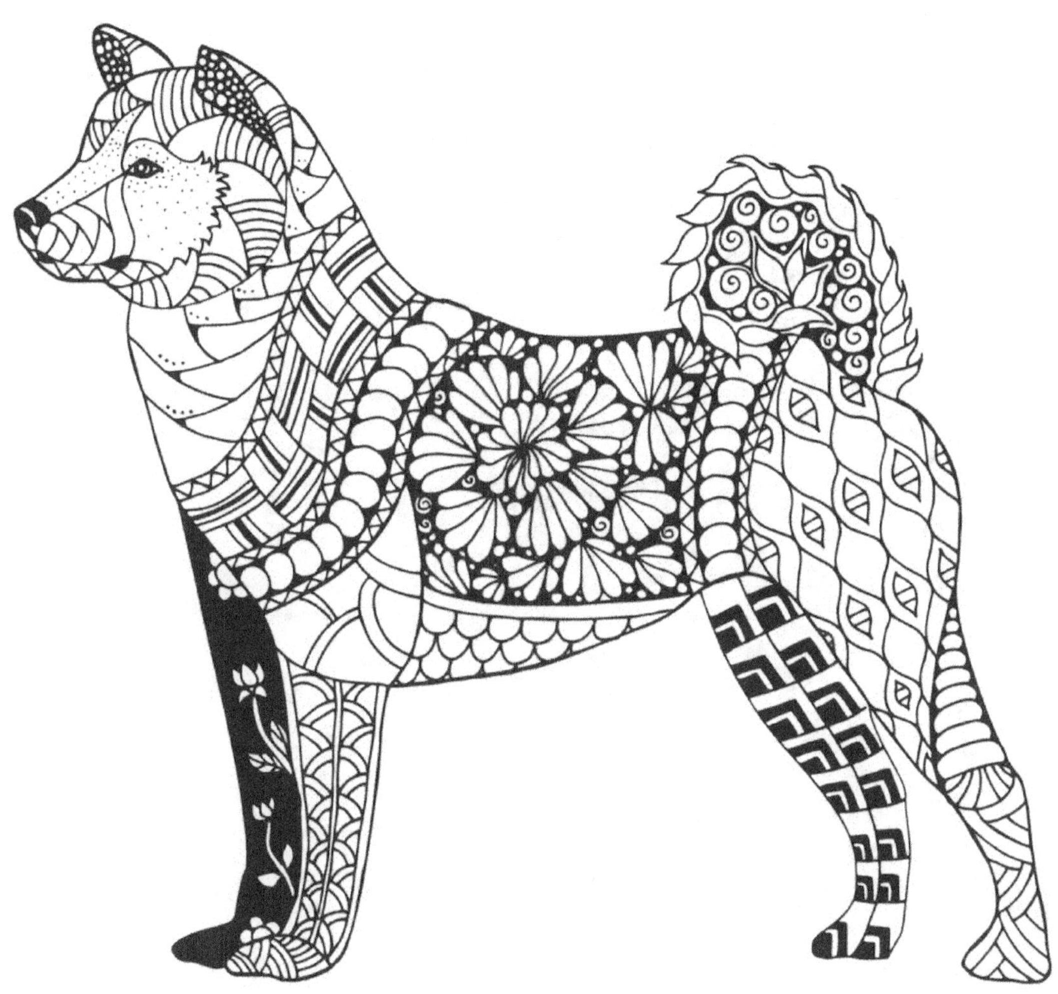

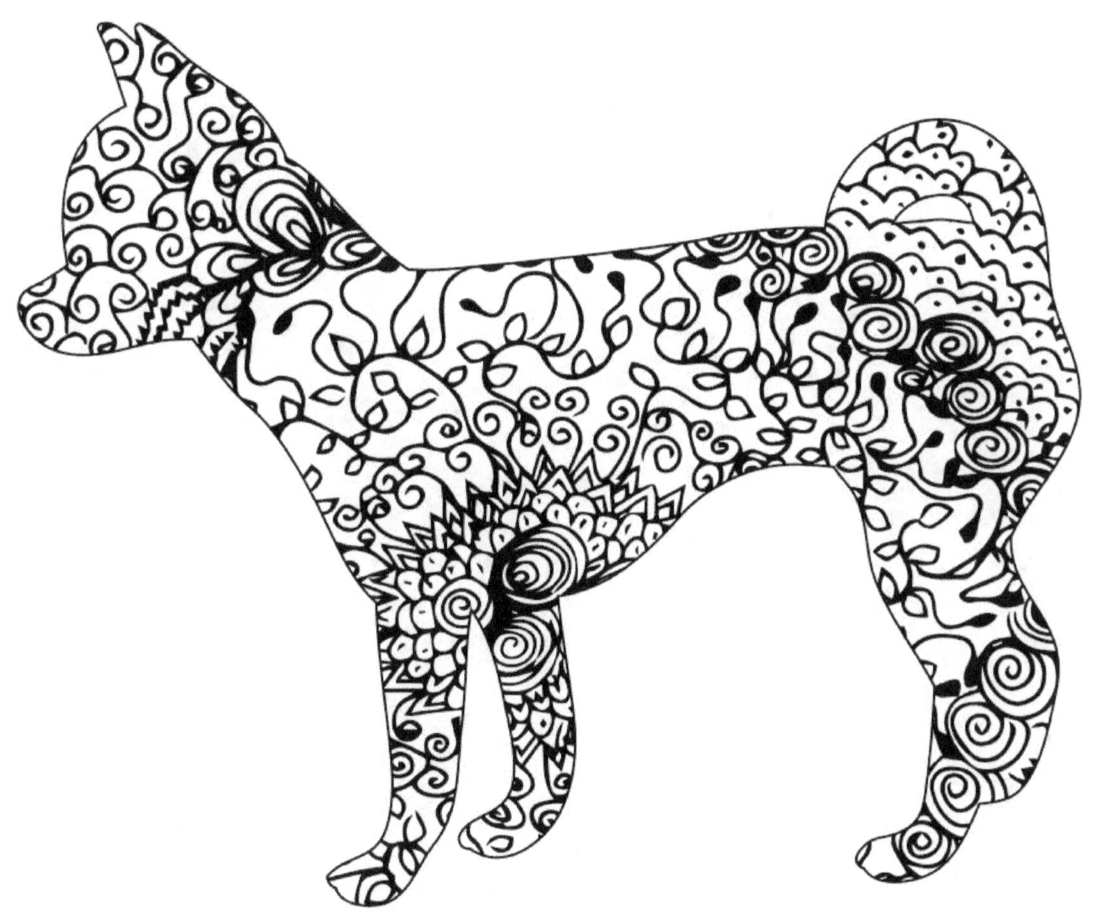

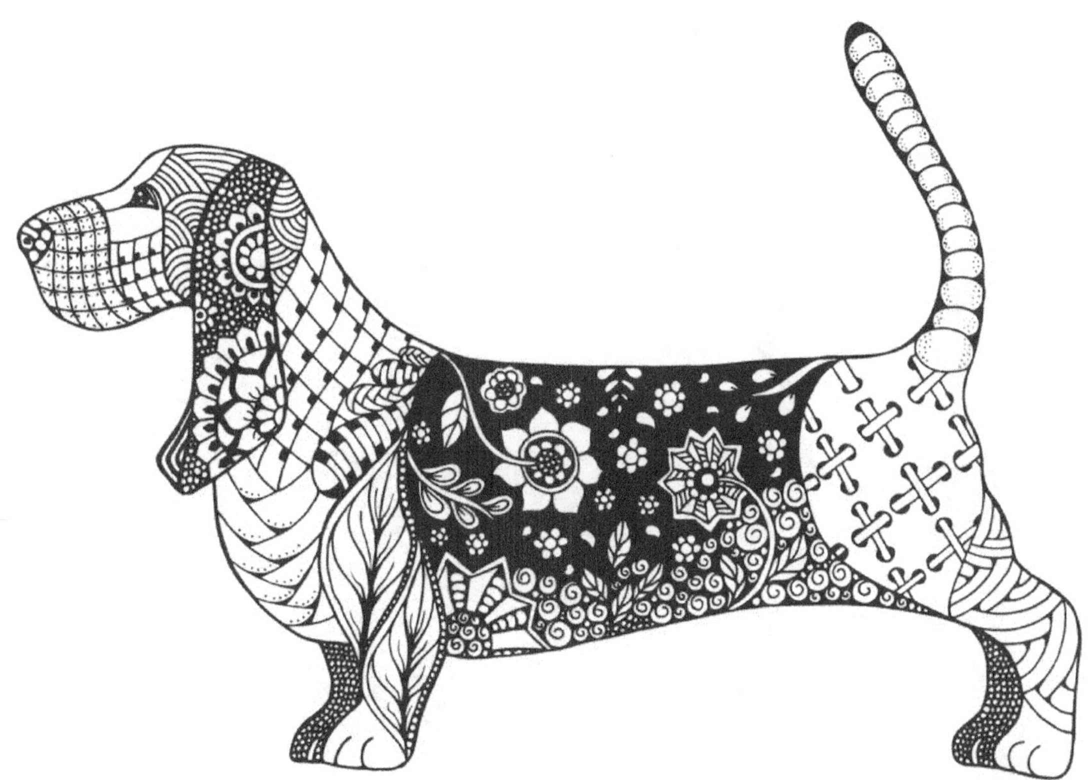

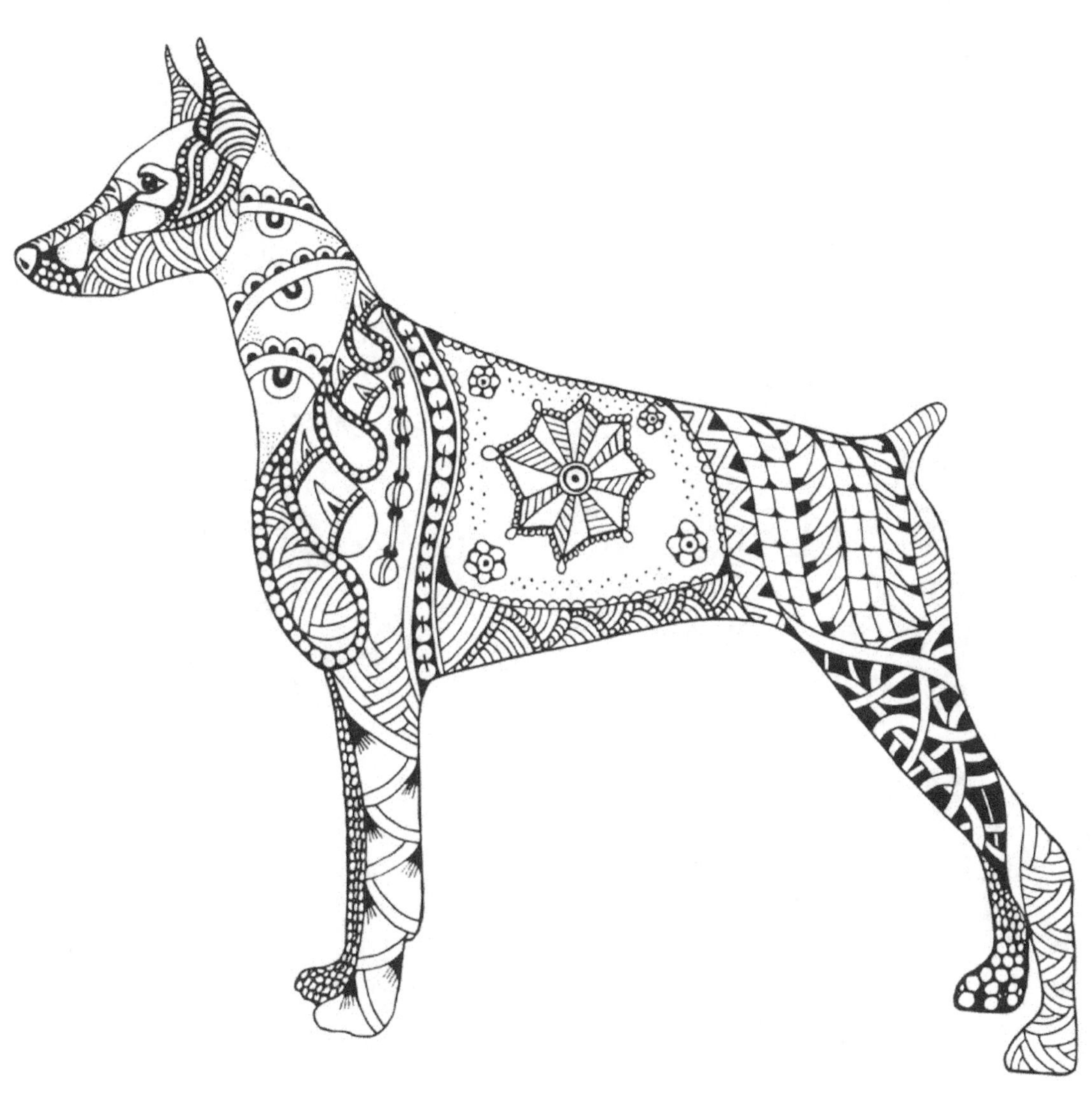

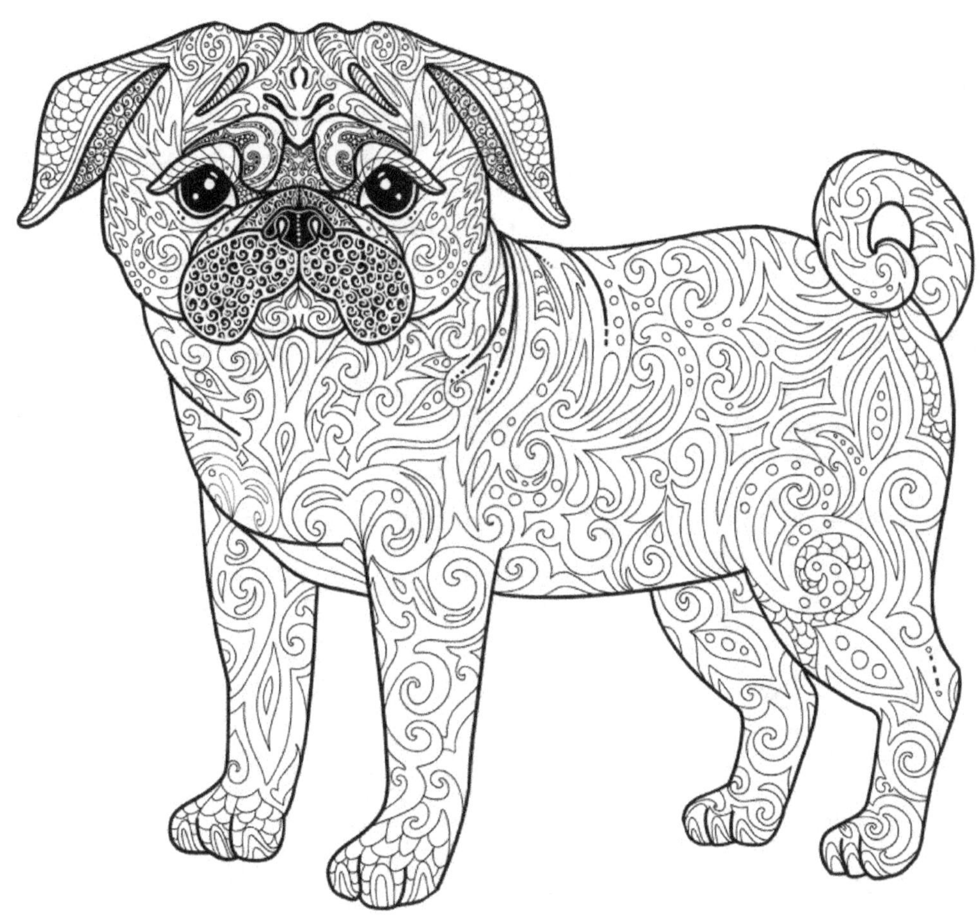

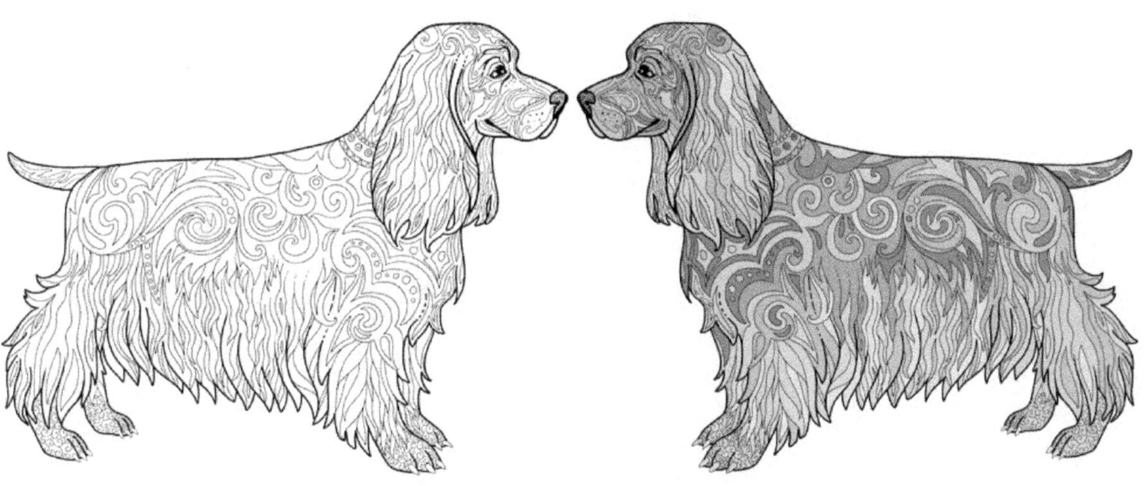

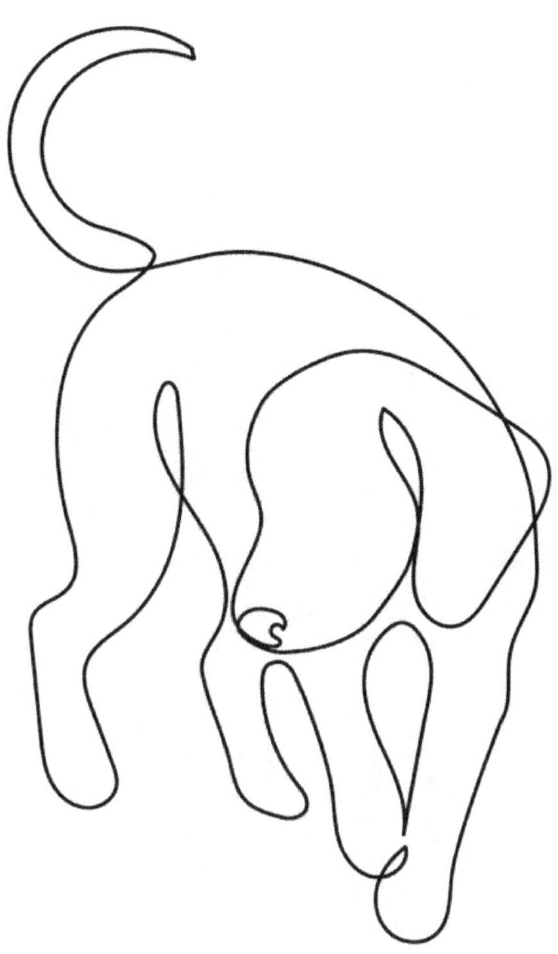

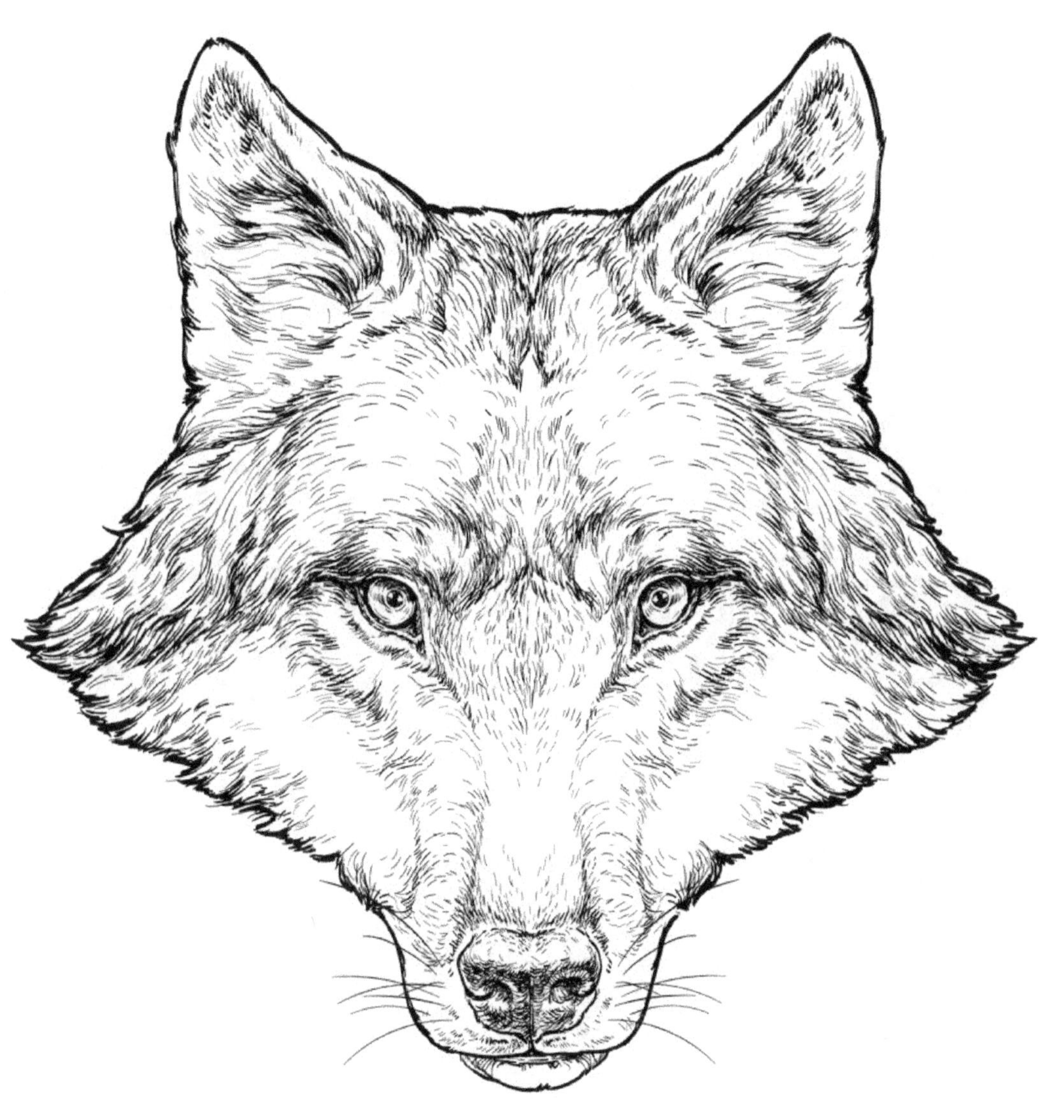

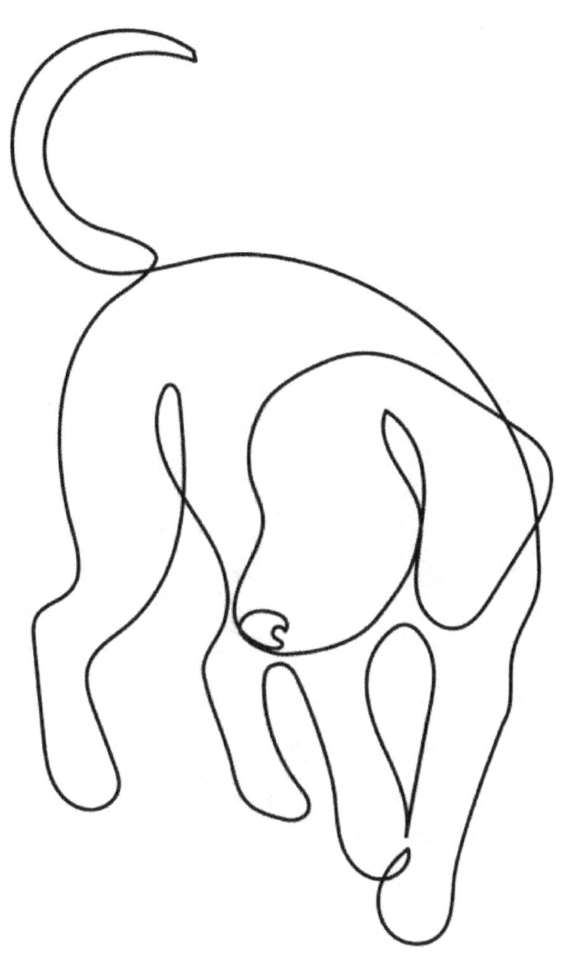

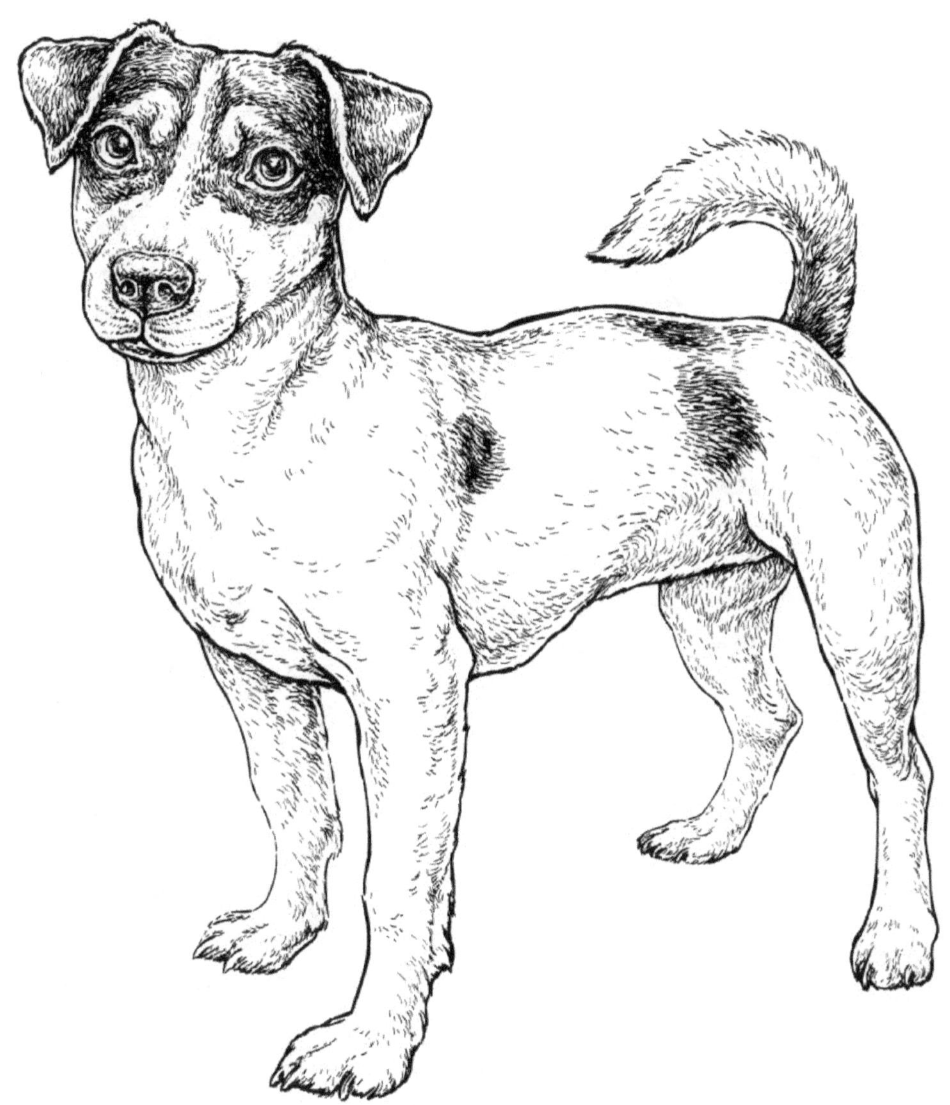

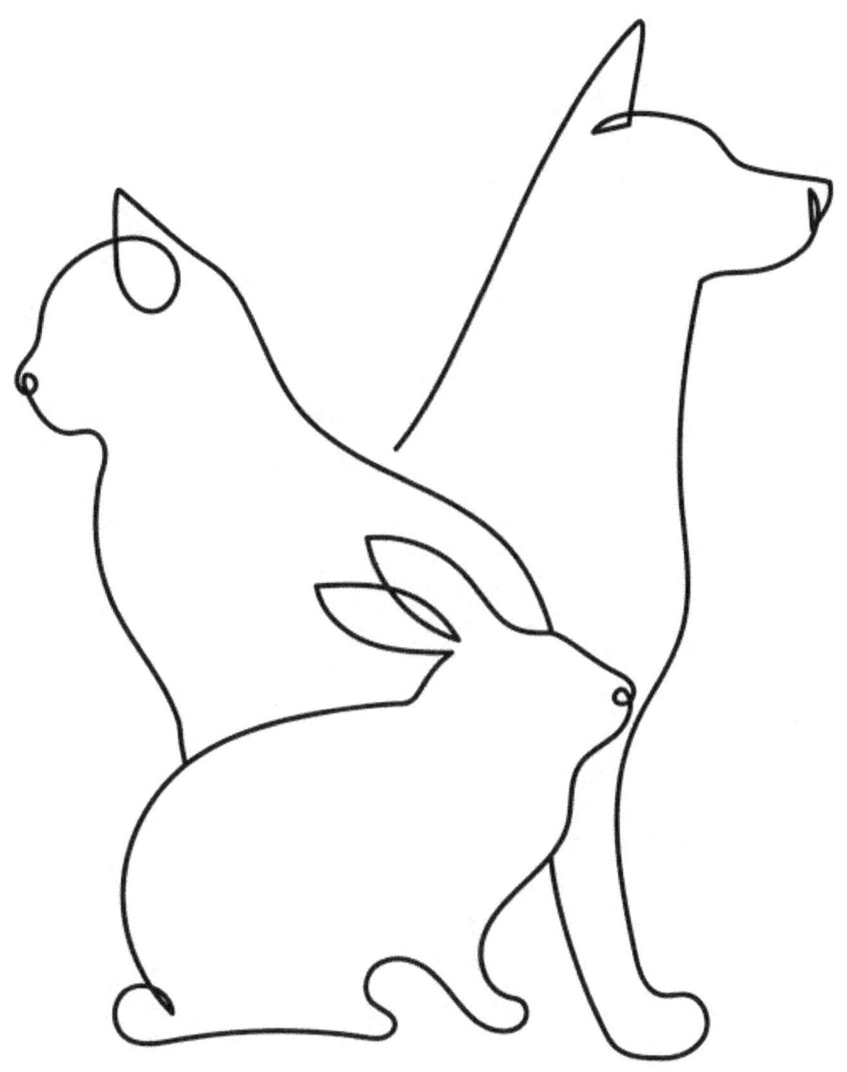

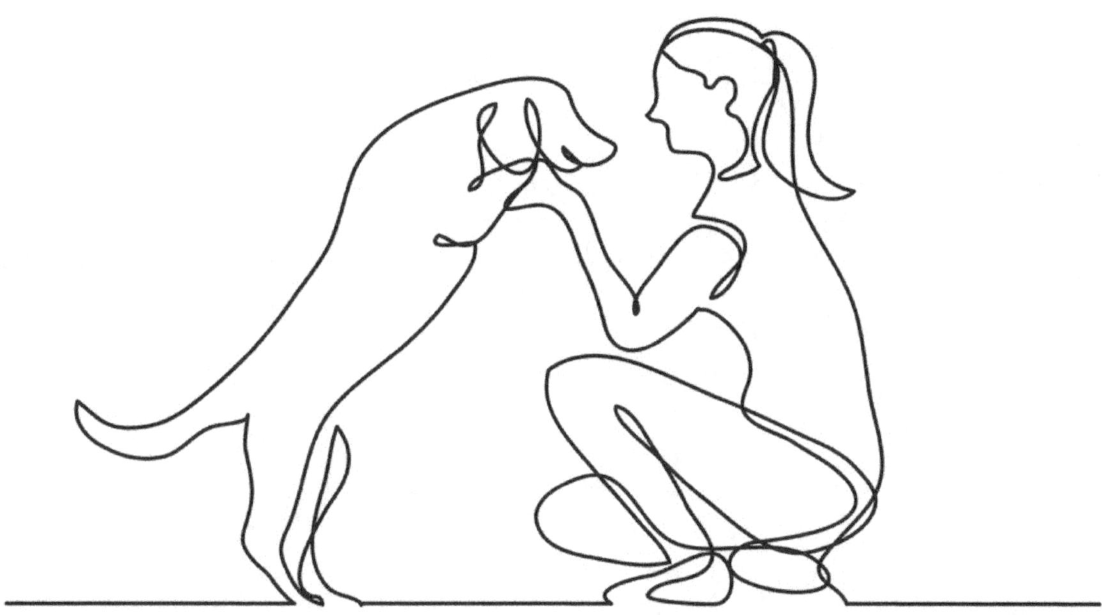

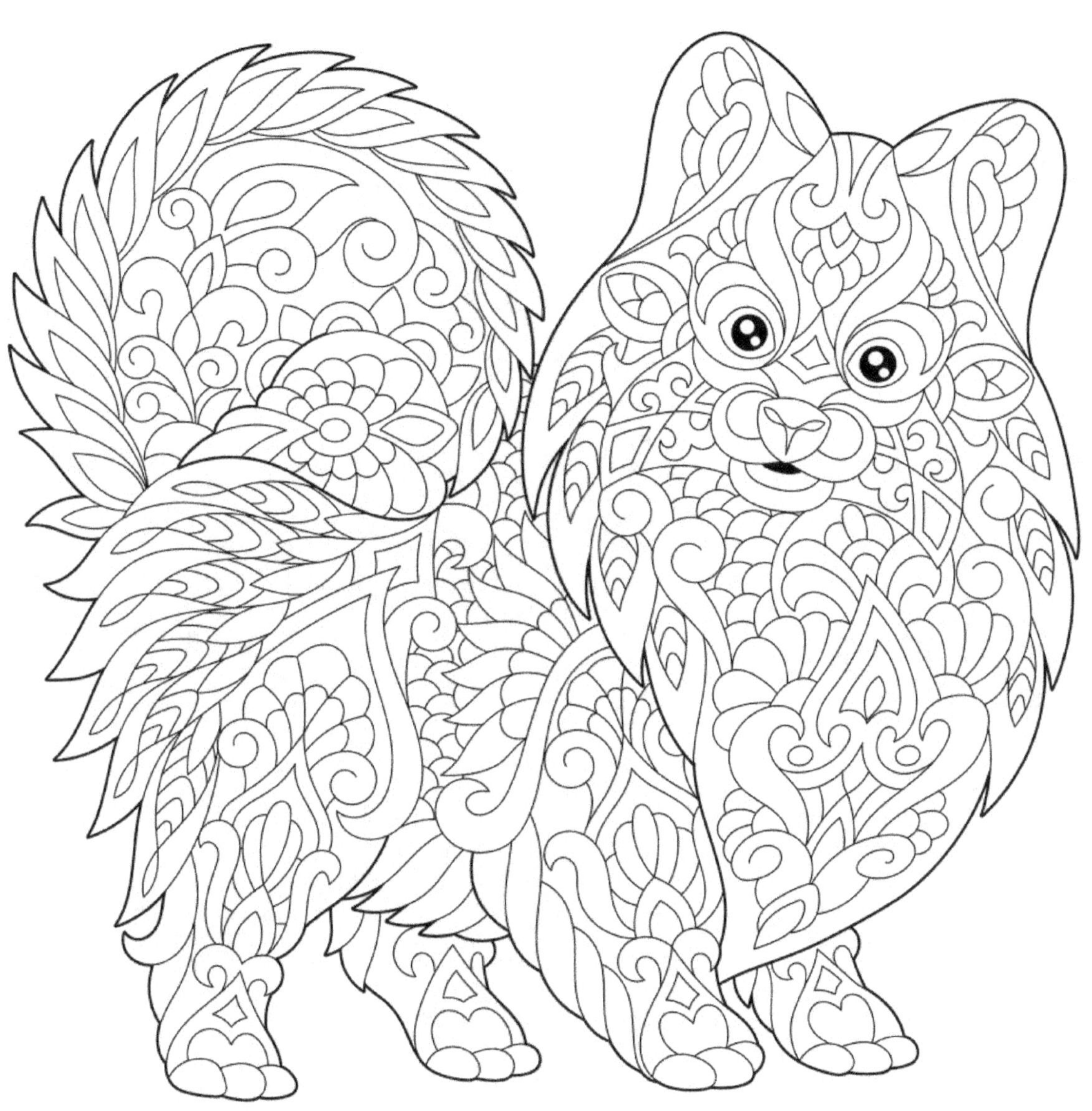

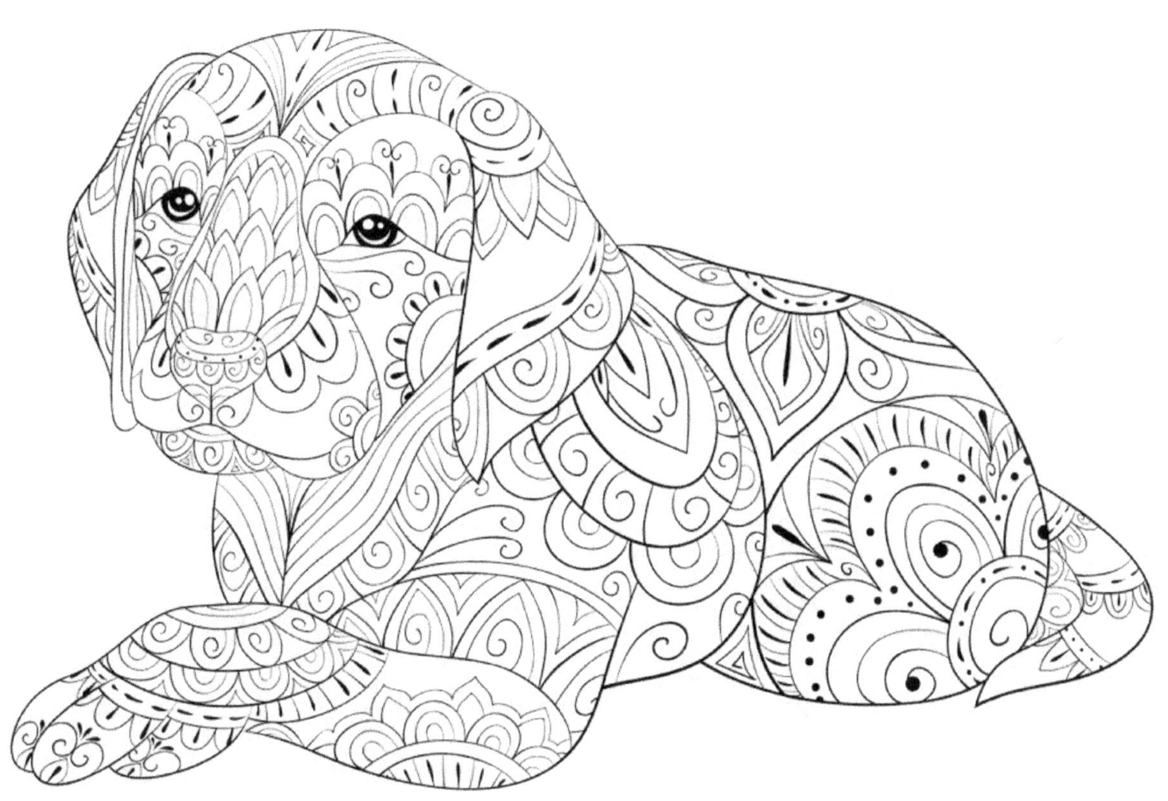